Intro

Grasslands are large areas of flat land with few trees and where some, but not much, rain falls.

Grasslands cover about a fifth of the Earth's land.

They are found all over the world except in Antarctica.

Grassland is also called fields, prairie and savanna.

Wham! Grasslands

A Killer Food Chain

by

Sean Callery

Illustrated by Shona Grant

With special thanks to our reader:
Daniel Hall

First published in 2009 in Great Britain by
Barrington Stoke Ltd
18 Walker St, Edinburgh, EH3 7LP

www.barringtonstoke.co.uk

Title ISBN: 978-1-84299-700-0
Pack ISBN: 978-1-84299-786-4

Printed in Great Britain by The Charlesworth Group

Food chains

Every living thing is part of a food chain. Everything has to eat to stay alive. We humans are at the top of lots of chains. Nothing eats us – unless we are very unlucky!

This book is all about a grasslands food chain.

Wham! Goodbye Sun, hello Earth

The Sun's rays take 8 minutes to get to Earth. Plants need this light to help them to make food.

Plants also get food from things in the ground. Small creatures, like worms, eat the soil and what they poo out is good food for plants. Plants are important in the food chains because lots of creatures eat them.

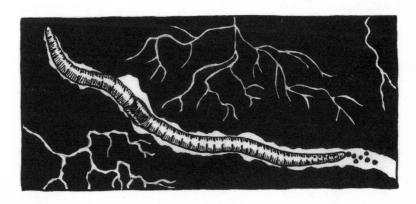

Wham! Goodbye plants, hello grasshopper

Grasshoppers are bad at flying but very good at jumping. They can leap a metre at a time.

They get their energy from the plants they eat.

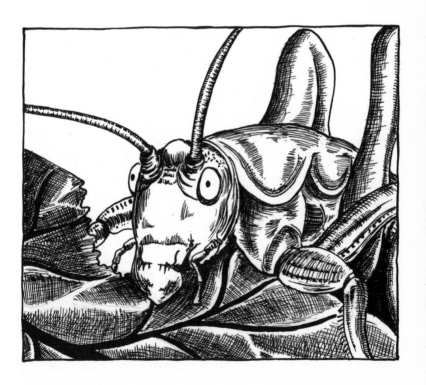

Could it kill me?

No, but a huge swarm of them could eat all the plants in a field and leave you without any food.

Wham! Goodbye grasshopper, hello toad

Toads can live on water or land. They catch their prey with their long, sticky tongues.

They gulp it down whole. They blink
hard to help the food go down.

Toads eat grasshoppers.

Could it kill me?

All toads have poison on their skin that can harm other creatures. Some toads can kill a dog, but you would only get a skin rash from them.

Wham! Goodbye toad, hello snake

The snake bites the toad and uses its fangs to inject poison called venom.

Then it eats the toad whole.

Could it kill me?

Yes! Some snake venom is strong enough to kill humans if they don't get help in time.

Wham! Goodbye snake, hello hawk

Hawks can see far better than us, and will dive on the snake from high above.

Could it kill me?

Birds of prey grip and stab their victims with their claws. Then they rip into the flesh with their sharp beaks.

They can't kill you, but they might eat
the meat from a dead body.

Wham! Goodbye hawk, hello soil

One day the hawk will die and slowly turn into dust.

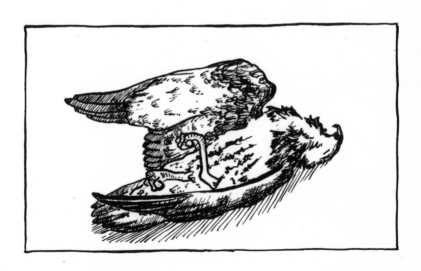

The dust goes into the soil and feeds the plant, and so the story starts again.

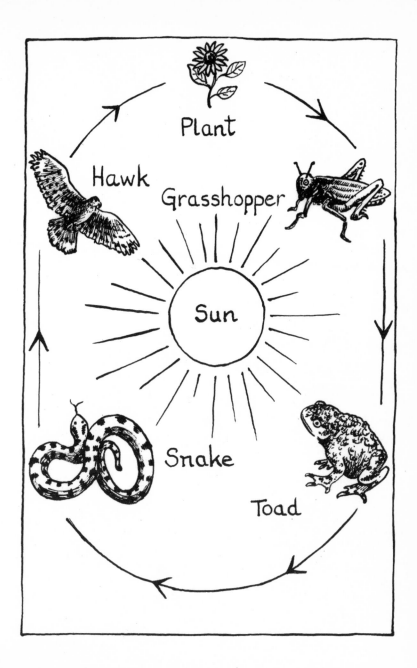

Wham! Fact file

Grasshoppers make noise by rubbing their back legs together.

If other animals attack them and eat them, toads swell up to make themselves too big to swallow.

Snake venom does not kill other snakes of the same type.

Some snakes spit their venom. They aim at the eyes of the attacking animal.

Hawks can see 8 times better than humans.

Like this book? Why not try the next one?

Wham! Undersea

Killer food chains deep under the sea!
Life under the sea is hard. Everything has to eat —
and everything gets eaten! From sea plants to
sharks, who comes out on top?

WHAM!

Watch out for more Wham! books ...

Wham! Arctic

Life in the Arctic is hard. Everything has to eat — and everything gets eaten! From krill to polar bears, who comes out on top?

Wham! Rainforest

Life in the rainforest is hard. Everything has to eat — and everything gets eaten! From poison dart frogs to jaguars, who comes out on top?

For more info check out our website:
www.barringtonstoke.co.uk